THE PEAKL ... WAY

BY

JOHN N. MERRILL

Maps and Photographs

by John N. Merrill

a J.N.M. PUBLICATION

1989

a J.N.M. PUBLICATION

JNM PUBLICATIONS,
WINSTER,
MATLOCK,
DERBYSHIRE.
DE4 2DQ

Conceived, edited, typeset, designed, marketed and distributed by John N. Merrill.

© Text and routes — John N. Merrill 1970 and 1989

© Maps and photographs — John N. Merrill 1989

First Published — December 1970
Reprinted three times.
This enlarged edition — April 1989

ISBN 0 907496 84 9

Meticulous research has been undertaken to ensure that this publication is highly accurate at the time of going to press. The publishers, however, cannot be held responsible for alterations, errors or omissions, but they would welcome notification of such for future editions.

Printed by: Elgar Printing Ltd

Set in Futura — medium and bold.

Front cover sketch — Stepping stones over the River Derwent near Hathersage — by John Creber. © JNM Publications. Back cover map © JNM Publications.

ABOUT JOHN N. MERRILL

John combines the characteristics and strength of a mountain climber with the stamina and athletic capabilities of a marathon runner. In this respect he is unique and has to his credit a whole string of remarkable long walks. He is without question the world's leading marathon walker.

Over the last fifteen years he has walked more than 100,000 miles and successfully completed ten walks of at least 1,000 miles or more.

His six major walks in Great Britain are -

Hebridean Journey .... 1,003 miles
Northern Isles Journey.. 913 miles
Irish Island Journey .... 1,578 miles
Parkland Journey.. 2,043 miles
Lands End to John o'Groats.. 1,608 miles

And in 1978 he became the first person (permanent Guinness Book of Records entry) to walk the entire coastline of Britain — 6,824 miles in ten months.

In Europe he has walked across Austria — 712 miles — hiked the Tour of Mont Blanc, completed High Level Routes in the Dolomites and Italian Alps, and the GR20 route across Corsica in training! In 1982 he walked across Europe — 2,806 miles in 107 days — crossing seven countries, the Swiss and French Alps and the complete Pyrennean chain — the hardest and longest mountain walk in Europe, with more than 600,000 feet of ascent!

In America he used the the world's longest footpath — The Appalachian Trail -2,200 miles — as a training walk. He has walked from Mexico to Canada via the Pacific Crest Trail in record time — 118 days for 2,700 miles. In Canada he has walked the Rideau Trail.

During the summer of 1984, John set off from Virginia Beach on the Atlantic coast, and walked 4,226 miles without a rest day, across the width of America to Santa Cruz and San Francisco on the Pacific Ocean. His walk is unquestionably his greatest achievement, being, in modern history, the longest, hardest crossing of the USA in the shortest time — under six months (178 days). The direct distance is 2,800 miles.

Between major walks John is out training in his own area — the Peak District National Park. As well as walking in other parts of Britain and Europe he has been trekking in the Himalayas five times. He has created more than ten challenge walks which have been used to raise more than £250,000 for charity. From his own walks he raised over £80,000. He is author of more than ninety books, most of which he publishes himself. His book sales are in excess of 2 million.

CONTENTS -

PEAKLAND WAY HIKERS AT ASHBOURNE

iv

INTRODUCTION -

Twenty years ago, in 1969, after studying maps and making intermittent walks in the Peak District, I set off one sunny August week to walk the Peakland Way for the first time. Three years later I walked it in four days during the depths of winter. These two contrasting circuits left me deeply impressed with the diversity of scenery in the National Park. I have walked it often since then, and for this book I completed my seventeenth circuit!

For a long while I felt the Peak District lacked a long walk which encompasses its many facets. I set about the task and attempted to combine all the varying beauty of the area — the limestone dales, the gritstone edges, the peat moorland plateaus, and the rural scenery with the enormous historical content of the region. I also wanted a walk that could be attempted by all, and decided 100 miles in a week was the right distance. I decided also that an average of about 12 miles a day allowed ample time to explore the area that is passed through during the day. As a result I ended up with the subject circular walk, with eight stages. At the end of each stage is a campsite, a Youth Hostel nearby, and in many cases a hotel or bed and breakfast — thus allowing anyone to walk it in the way he chooses, be he a backpacker, hosteller or walker.

Since 1969 I have had literally hundreds of letters from fellow Peakland Wayers — thankfully all complimentary! I am biased, but, despite all my walking around the world I still enjoy walking the Peakland Way. Here in one fell swoop you see and enjoy one of the finest inland scenic areas of England. I hope you enjoy your circuit, and perhaps I may meet you on your walk.
In any event — HAPPY WALKING!

John N. Merrill.
Winster. 1989.

1

HOW TO DO IT

The route is covered by the following Ordnance Survey maps:-

1" Tourist Map — The Peak District

1:25,000 Series — Outdoor Leisure Map — The White Peak
- The Dark Peak

1:25,000 Pathfinder Series Sheets Nos SK28/38 — Sheffield and No SK04/14 –
Ashbourne and the Churnet Valley.

1:50,000 Series — Sheet No. 110 — Sheffield and Huddersfield
- Sheet No. 119 — Buxton, Matlock and Dovedale

From the many letters I have had from people who have walked the entire route
the majority walk it in eight days. A few have completed it within four days, whil
others have done sections over successive weekends. There are no rules c
regulations as to how you should walk it. The walk is simply devised for you to enjo
a good walk through delightful scenery.

I have based the route on backpacking, and this appears to be the most popula
way of doing it. At the end of each stage there is a campsite, but nearby are gues
houses or hostels where you can stay. This means you can walk the route and carr
little weight whilst staying in houses or hostels. It also means if the weather is roug
there is always somewhere nearby to dry out.

The summer months — May to September — are the best months to walk the route
with long daylight hours and kind weather. In winter it is an interesting walk
especially in snow! But you do have the advantage of having the countryside t
yourself. The whole route uses rights of way, with the occasional road to link it a
together. Some of the paths are popular, such as the Kinder and gritstone edg
sections, but the vast majority of the route is along quieter paths, some still hardl
defineable. From my walking notes and maps you should have no difficulty i
finding your way round.

A master record of fellow walkers of the Peakland Way is kept by me at JNM
Publications, Winster, Matlock, Derbyshire, DE4 2DQ. Completion certificates an
badges are available for the successful. An annual get together of all John Merri
walk guide walkers is held in November each year.

ABOUT THE WALK -

Whilst every care is taken detailing and describing the walks in this book, it should be borne in mind that the countryside changes by the seasons and the work of man. I have described the walks to the best of my ability, detailing what I have found on the walk in the way of stiles and signs. Obviously with the passage of time stiles become broken or replaced by a ladder stile or even a small gate. Signs too have a habit of being broken or pushed over. All the routes follow rights of way and only on rare occasions will you have to overcome obstacles in its path, such as a barbed wire fence or electric fence.

The seasons bring occasional problems whilst out walking which should also be borne in mind. In the height of summer paths become overgrown and you will have to fight your way through in a few places. In low lying areas the fields are often full of crops, and although the pathline goes straight across it may be more practical to walk round the field edge to get to the next stile or gate. In summer the ground is generally dry but in autumn and winter, especially because of our climate, the surface can be decidedly wet and slippery; sometimes even glutonous mud!

These comments are part of countryside walking which help to make your walk more interesting or briefly frustrating. Standing in a farmyard up to your ankles in mud might not be funny at the time but upon reflection was one of the highlights of the walk!

WALKING IN THE MANIFOLD VALLEY

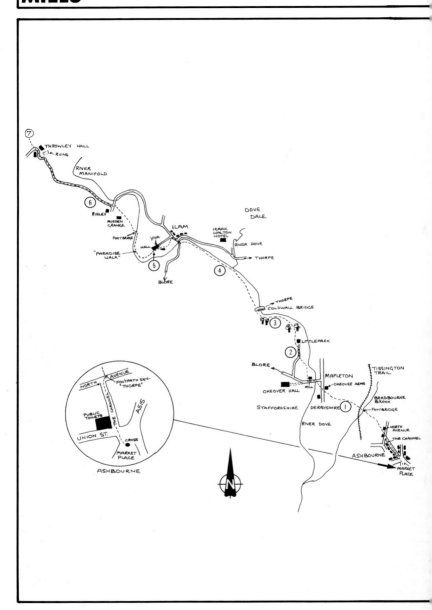

ASHBOURNE — Full of historical buildings, notably the Church and Church Street, the most complete 17th Century street in Britain. Ashbourne is famous for its unique football game and for 'Gingerbread men'.

SHBOURNE TO WETTONMILL — 10 MILES

MAPS — 1:25,000 Outdoor Leisure Map — The White Peak — West heet.
1:25,000 Pathfinder Series Sheet No SK04/14 — Ashbourne and he Churnet Valley.

WALKING INSTRUCTIONS -

After giving the Market Cross a hefty slap, leave the Market Place via the top lefthandside and cross Union Street to 'The Channel' on the immediate right of the public conveniences. Ascend the cobbled path past the houses to the road at the top — North Avenue. Cross over, and as signposted — 'Footpath to Thorpe' — follow the fenced path to a stile. Turn right before descending to your left to the footbridge over the brook. Keep to the path on your right, signposted for Mapleton, and shortly ascend steps and cross the Tissington Trail. Descend further steps to a kissing gate and ascend the field beyond to a stile. Continue ascending, now gradually keeping straight ahead. Over the brow of the hill you descend via the stiles. As you near Mapleton village turn right across the field and gain the village via a fenced path, coming out onto the road to the left of the Okeover Arms.

Cross the road to the right and, as footpath signposted — 'Dovedale' — cross the field to the River Dove and road. Turn left over the bridge and enter Staffordshire. 200 yards later, just before the entrance gates to Okeover Hall, turn right as footpath signposted — 'Coldwall Bridge 1½ miles' and 'Ilam 2½ miles'. First you walk close to the mill stream on your right before reaching the River Dove. Here you leave the waterside and cross the field to your left to a stile and farm track. Turn right along the track towards Littlepark. Just before it bear left around the buildings, and once over the crest of the field you descend to a small wood and the River Dove. Cross the stiles and leave the riverside for ½ a mile to another small wood. Here you rejoin the river and ½ mile later reach Coldwall Bridge.

Continue ahead across the fields, and you soon rejoin the riverside to reach Ilam a mile away. Turn right over the bridge before turning left towards the entrance to Ilam Hall. Here turn left and left again at the entrance to Dovedale House, and follow the path to Ilam Church and on to Ilam Hall (YHA) and its tearoom and National Trust Information Centre. Turn left and descend the steps to the River Manifold. Turn right and follow the well-used path along 'Paradise Walk'. After ½ mile cross the footbridge on your left and bear right along the stiled path to the right of Musden Grange. Upon gaining the single track road, turn left then right almost immediately and follow the road for the next 1½ miles to Throwley Hall. Walk through the farm and turn right then left immediately afterwards to the stile and path up the field to the narrow plantation and ladder stile. Cross through the wood, and ahead is an enjoyable view up Manifold Valley and the impressive Beeston Tor.

MAPLETON — 18th Century aisle-less church. Okeover Hall dates from the 17th Century.

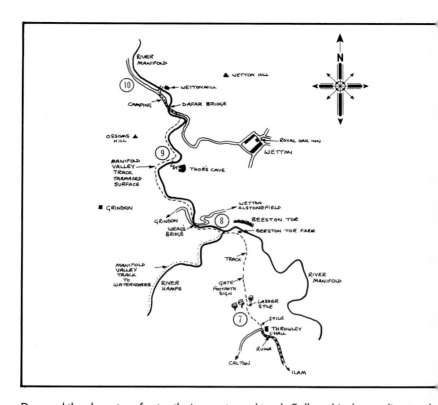

Descend the slope to a footpath sign, gate and track. Follow this descending track to the River Manifold and the line of the old Leek and Manifold Light Railway, which ceased in 1932. Continue ahead on the tarmaced path. Cross the road at Weag's Bridge and follow the tarmaced path along the Manifold Valley to Wettonmill 1½ miles away. En route you pass below the majestic Thor's Cave on your right. That ends the first section, and the nearest pub is at Wetton (The Royal Oak) a little over a mile away!

COLDWALL BRIDGE — Built in 1726 and part of an old coaching road. On the Thorpe side can be seen a milestone — 'Cheadle 11 miles".

ILAM — Church was built in 1611 and has funeral garlands, St. Bertram's tomb, and a monument to David Pike Watts, who once resided at the Hall. The Hall dates from 1842 and was built by Jesse Watts Russell in Victorian Gothic Revival style. It is National Trust property and includes a Youth Hostel. The Hall is reputedly haunted.

BEESTON TOR — Limestone buttress more than 200 feet high and wide. In St. Bertram's Cave at its base 50 Saxon coins were found in 1924. Other caves have yielded bones from lynx, polecat and reindeer. The buttress is now a popular climbing ground.

THOR'S CAVE — Reached by a steep path, but one of the most impressive limestone caves anywhere. Extensively excavated early this century, and finds proved the cave was occupied by man in the first centuries A.D..

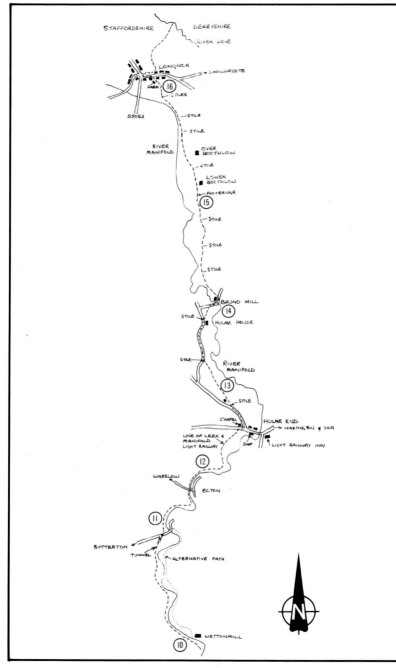

WETTONMILL TO BLACKWELL — 14 MILES

MAP — O.S. 1:25,000 Outdoor Leisure Map — The White Peak — West Sheet.

WALKING INSTRUCTIONS

Continue along the lefthand side of the valley, on the tarmaced line, which now serves as the road to Wettonmill. After 1 1/4 miles you enter the old railway tunnel. At the end keep straight ahead on the railway line, which is now closed to vehicle traffic. If you want to walk in quieter terrain, instead of walking on the left of the valley from Wettonmill, you can walk along the old road on the right which brings you out to the road just beyond the tunnel. You will have to turn left and right shortly afterwards to rejoin the route proper. From the tunnel carry on along the 'railway line' to Hulme End 1 1/2 miles away.

On reaching the B5054 road turn right, (Just ahead on your right is a shop and campsite and inn) and by a chapel on the left shortly afterwards, turn left along the road. After 1/4 mile you will find a stile on your right. It is not obvious in the hedge. Cross the stile and aim for the right of the building where there is a stile. Cross this and keep to the field boundary on your right. After the second field you keep the boundary on your left. 1/4 mile later you reach the minor road. Turn right and 1/3 mile later, just past Hulme House, turn right via the stile and cross the field to the bridge over the Manifold and Brund Mill, a former cornmill.

Walk past the Mill and other buildings on your left. Almost opposite the road to Brund on your right is the stile and path on your left for Longnor. The stile is small, but once you have crossed the first field to the stile, where you turn right, the stiles and path line become more discernible. First you walk with a wall on your right before descending to the River Manifold. The stile near here is at the end of the wall. Continue ahead and rejoin the river on entering the third field. Here you leave the river to a stile in the hedge on your right. You now cross four fields to Pool Farm. Pass the farm on the immediate lefthandside by a stile and descend to a small footbridge. Continue straight ahead across another field to a walled track on the immediate left of a cottage. Cross the track and continue across the fields to Lower Boothlow Farm. At the end of the next field you bear left and begin angling your way to the banks of the River Manifold. The whole section is well stiled. After five fields you leave the river by turning right to the stile and ascending to Folds End Farm, track and Longnor. Walk up the track to the main road and turn left to Longnor Market Place.

LEEK AND MANIFOLD VALLEY LIGHT RAILWAY — Running through the valley from Hulme End to Waterhouses was this railway. The line was officially opened in 1904 and cost £4,000 per mile to construct. It was never a financial success, partly because being in the valley it was far from the villages and partly because the mining and milk trades declined. In 1934 it was closed and the Staffordshire County Council converted it to a pedestrian walkway.

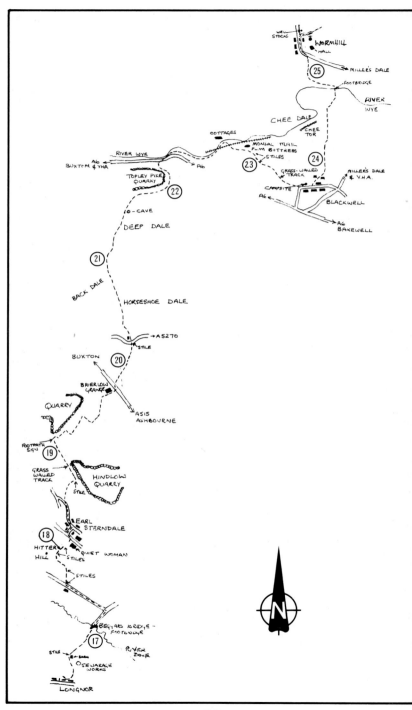

WELL
STOCKS

WORMHILL
HALL

25

MILLER'S DALE

FOOTBRIDGE

CHEE DALE

RIVER
WYE

COTTAGES

CHEE
TOR

MONSAL TRAIL
PLUM BUTTRESS
STILES

24

RIVER WYE

A6
BUXTON & YHA

A6

23

GRASS-WALLED
TRACK

MILLER'S DALE
& Y.H.A.

TOPLEY PIKE
QUARRY

22

CAMPSITE

A6

BLACKWELL

A6 ←

O-CAVE

DEEP DALE

A6
BAKEWELL

21

BACK DALE

HORSESHOE DALE

→ A5270

STILE

BUXTON

20

BRIERLOW
GRANGE

A515
ASHBOURNE

QUARRY

FOOTPATH
SIGN

19

GRASS
WALLED
TRACK

HINDLOW
QUARRY

STILE

EARL
STERNDALE

18

HITTER
HILL

QUIET WOMAN

STILES

STILES

BEGGARS BRIDGE -
FOOTBRIDGE

STILE

17

RIVER
DOVE

SEWARAGE
WORKS

LONGNOR

N

Exit the Market Place via Chapel Street. Turn right past the Church and take the second lane on your left, beside a wooden building, and ascend out of the village. Turn left at the top and right soon afterwards and descend the track. At the bottom turn left in front of the barn to the stile on its immediate lefthandside. Cross the field beyond to an abandoned well. Just over the field brow you descend to the footbridge — Beggar's Bridge — over the River Derwent. Here you step back into Derbyshire. Ascend the walled grass track beyond and at the tarmaced lane turn left along it. After ½ mile, beside the second building, turn right and ascend the field. At the top turn left and continue ascending the valley side to a stile close to the summit of Hitter Hill. Turn right and descend two fields to the Quiet Woman Inn and village of Earl Sterndale.

Ascend past the church and turn left along the road. After ¼ mile leave the road and ascend the steep slope. At the top you gain a walled grass track. Turn left and follow this for the next ½ mile; on your right is Hindlow Quarry. Turn right, as footpath signposted, and descend the fields on the immediate right of another limestone quarry. The whole path here is very well stiled and signposted around the field edges. Cross the line of an old railway line and follow another on your left towards Brierlow Grange (B. & B.), turning right after ¼ mile to get there. Walk past the farm to the A515 road. Turn left and right almost immediately afterwards and cross the stone stile. The stile is partly hidden by the trees and is beneath the road. Cross the field beyond before descending to a stile at a bend in the A5270 road. Cross the road and enter Horseshoe Dale.

Continue along the floor of the dale, and after ½ mile you pass Back Dale on your left. You now enter Deep Dale, with rugged cliffs and interesting caves. The path now keeps to the righthandside on the dale floor. In a little over one mile you reach the spoil heaps and lagoon of Topley Pike Quarry. Keep to the right and descend the path to the dale floor. Here turn left, passing the quarry buildings on your left. In the final stages you descend the quarry road to the A6 road and footpath sign. Cross the road and walk down the track beside the River Wye and the approaches of Chee Dale. After walking under your third railway arch, a little over ½ mile down the road, turn right and cross the railway — now the Monsal Trail — via a bridge. Continue walking up a shallow dale for 50 yards before turning left and ascending the dale side. At the top you come to a stile, and these stiles guide you across four fields to a walled grass track ¼ mile away. Walk along this track, then follow the road into the hamlet of Blackwell. As you enter, notice the path and sign for Wormhill on your left — this is the start of the next section.

LONGNOR — Very attractive gritstone village with cobbled market place. The church was rebuilt in 1780 in classical style and has a false ceiling. Amongst the gravestones can be seen one to the local blacksmith and one to William Billinge. He was a remarkable man, having fought in numerous battles; he died in 1791 aged 112.

EARL STERNDALE — The inn is called 'The Quiet Woman' and the sign depicts a headless woman, with the words — 'Soft words turneth away wrath'. It is said that a former landlady was a constant chatterbox and eventually the locals could stand it no more. They gave permission for the landlord to decapitate her, which he did!

LONGNOR MARKET PLACE TOLLS

WORMHILL STOCKS

QUIET WOMAN INN, EARL STERNDALE

HOPE CROSS

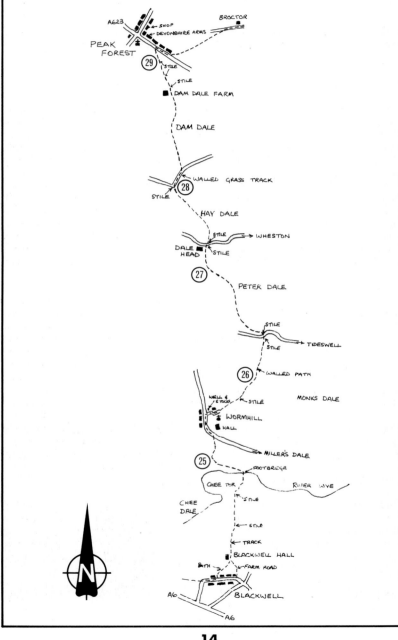

BLACKWELL TO BARBER BOOTH — 12 MILES

MAPS — O.S. 1:25,000 Outdoor Leisure Maps — The White Peak (West sheet) and the Dark Peak.

WALKING INSTRUCTIONS

Leave Blackwell either by the path on its western side to Blackwell Hall Farm or by the farm road on the eastern side. Walk through the farm on the track, heading due north. At the end of the second field you turn right then left and walk beside a wall on your left, now having left the track. At the end of the field where there is a stile you begin the descent to the River Wye and Chee Dale. The path zig-zags its way down to the footbridge. Cross and ascend the dale side to your left on a well-defined path. After 1/4 mile the path swings (right) northwards and you soon reach a track which leads you to the road close to Wormhill. Turn left and walk through the small village to the first road on your right; the stocks and Brindley Well are just ahead. Turn right along the road, passing Wormhill Church on your right. Just beyond you keep straight on a footpath which first crosses a large narrow field to a tree and stile. Bear left and begin descending a walled path, which you follow for a little over 1/4 mile. Just after the end of the walled path you reach the minor road to Tideswell in front of Peter Dale.

Cross the road and walk up Peter Dale. 1 1/4 miles later cross the minor road close to Dale Head and continue along the path now in Hay Dale. 1/2 mile later, cross a stile and turn right along a walled grass track. 150 yards later leave it and follow the path through Dam Dale, your third and last dale on this section. Keep to the righthand side of Dam Dale Farm. Keep straight ahead and the stiles will guide you all the way to Peak Forest village. On your left is the Devonshire Arms. A little further on the road to your to Old Dam is the shop. At the A623 road turn right, and, immediately past the last house on your left, turn left and follow the path to Broctor. For the first two fields you keep the wall on your right. After ascending a stile, the wall is now on your left. At the road turn right, and 150 yards later left up the road to The Cop. Here on your right is the path, stile and footpath sign for the route across Old Moor. Follow this across, keeping the stone wall on your left all the way. After a mile you reach the walled track and junction of footpaths. Turn left and keep on the walled track for the next mile. After a short distance the track bears right and leads you past Rowter Farm (campsite).

WORMHILL — Brindley Well was built in 1875 in memory of James Brindley, who was born in the parish in 1716. Despite no schooling, he became renowned for his canal building. The old village stocks are nearby. The church dedicated to St. Margaret has an interesting tower, being a replica of the Saxon tower at Stomping in Sussex. Wormhill Hall dates from Elizabethan times and is owned by the historic Derbyshire family — the Bagshawes.

MONSAL TRAIL — Former railway line from Matlock to Buxton. Part of it has recently been converted to a pedestrian way between Chee Dale and Bakewell -— 8 miles. The tunnels have been closed, and link paths join the trail together.

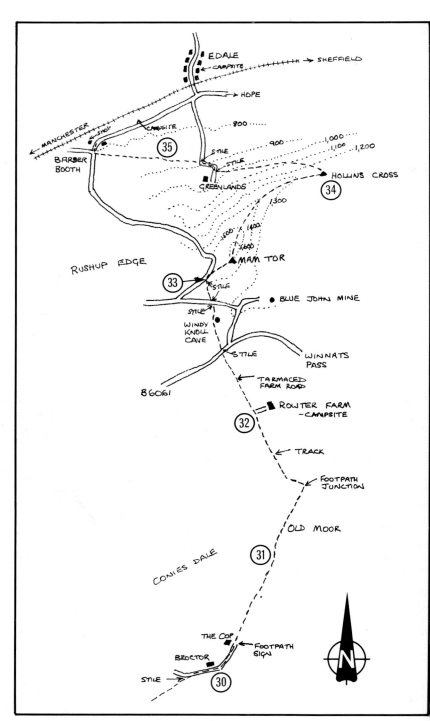

Beyond the farm entrance the now tarmaced track leads you to the B6061 road. Cross the road to the stile and path heading for Windy Knoll (the cave is just to your right) and the A625 road. All the time your objective — Mam Tor — acts as a guide. Cross the road to another stile and ascend the path to the road at Mam Nick. Turn right and follow the well-used path to the summit of Mam Tor — one of the finest viewpoints in the Peak District. Keep to the ridge and follow the path for the next 3/4 mile to the monument at Hollins Cross. Here turn left and begin descending. On your right is Kinder and Edale — tomorrow's route. After 100 yards turn left and follow the path, angling due west across the slopes. After 1/2 mile you reach the minor road to Greenlands. Turn right down it, and after crossing a small stream and where the road turns sharp right, ascend the stile and cross further fields to Barber Booth 3/4 mile away. Turn right at the road for the village. Also a short distance along the Edale road is a campsite, and Edale village and facilities is a mile away.

PEAK FOREST — One of the most historically interesting villages in the Peak District. Was once part of the Royal Forest of the Peak. The church was built in 1880 on the site of a small chapel that was pulled down. The chapel became renowned in the Midlands as a Gretna Green. Between 1728 — 1754 as many as 100 'run away' marriages were solemnised here. Even today it is quite in order for a couple to be married here without banns. The only stipulation is that one of them must live in the village for fifteen days prior to the service.

MAM TOR — An impressive vantage point over the Hope Valley. The summit has extensive earthworks — ditches and ridges — which are the remains of an Iron Age fort dating from about 1180 B.C..

WINDY KNOLL CAVE — A small entrance leads down into a large chamber. This was extensively excavated last century, and bison and deer remains were found. A total of 6,800 bones and 500 teeth were uncovered. Some of the finds can be seen in Sheffield and Buxton Museums.

17

BARBER BOOTH TO HAGG FARM — 14 MILES

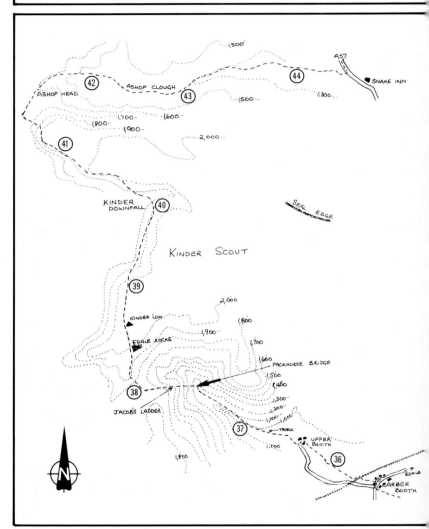

BARBER BOOTH TO HAGG FARM — 14 MILES

MAP — O.S. 1:25,000 Outdoor Liesure Map — The Dark Peak.

WALKING INSTRUCTIONS

The toughest day of the route, but the most enjoyable through rugged moorland. Just past the shop in Barber Booth turn left along the lane and cross the railway line. Immediately afterwards turn left, and after 100 yards turn right and cross the well-stiled fields to the righthand side of Upper Booth, a little over half a mile away. Entering the farmyard turn left to the road. Here turn right and follow the road then track past Lee House and onto the packhorse bridge at the foot of Jacob's Ladder. You are walking along the route of the Alternative Path of the Pennine Way.

All the time from Barber Booth the high ramparts of Kinder have dominated the scene. You now begin ascending in earnest as you follow the distinct path up Jacob's Ladder. At the top of the steep section you have a walled path to follow — a former packhorse route. After 1/3 mile take the path to your right up to a gritstone wall and the perimeter of the Kinder plateau. Turn right and walk beside the wall on a good path for 200 yards. Turn left and aim for the righthand side of Edale Rocks. The pathline is faint through the peat groughs, and in bad weather a compass is essential. From the gritstone rocks cross more peat to the triangulation pillar on Kinder Low. Continue ahead to the plateau's perimeter, where you find a well-used path heading almost due north to Kinder Downfall, 1 1/4 miles away.

Cross the Kinder River above the Downfall and continue around the perimeter (to your left) on the well-used path for the next 1 1/2 miles. Here at the north-western edge of the plateau you descend sharply to Ashop Head. Turn right, now leaving the Pennine Way, and follow the path down Ashop Clough to the Snake road, Inn and Camping Barn 3 1/2 miles away. You keep to the lefthand side of the clough, and in the final stages after passing through a small plantation you cross a footbridge and ascend to the A57 road. The Inn is 200 yards to your right.

PACKHORSE ROUTES — Jacob's Ladder is a former route over the moorland to Hayfield, passing Edale Cross. The name Jacob's Ladder originates from a packhorse driver who lived locally. Every time he ascended this steep section he cut another step, eventually making a 'ladder of steps'. The path you follow beyond the Snake road is also a former packhorse route known as Doctor's Gate, which ran from Glossop to the Hope Valley.

KINDER — Remote, barren moorland area approximately 2,000 feet above sea level. Fine in good weather, but in bad conditions can prove extremely tough.. Needs respect even in summer. The 'downfall' is an impressive waterfall: in summer the fall is often blown back onto the moorland, and in winter the fall is a quivering cascade of ice and a popular climb.

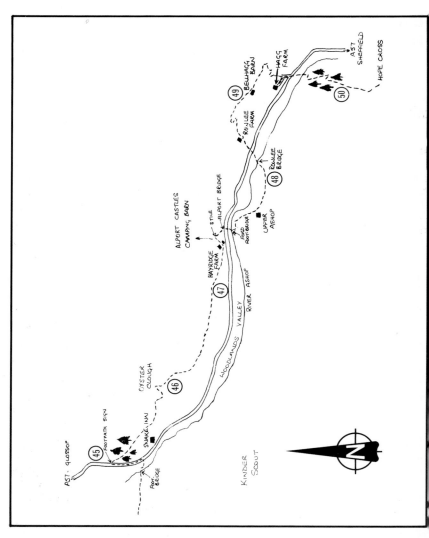

PACKHORSE BRIDGE AT START OF JACOB'S LADDER

At the road — A57 — turn left and walk up it for ¼ mile to the path sign on your right. Turn right and ascend through the trees on a good path. After ten minutes you reach open country; keep to the path and follow it as it curves down to Oyster Clough and then around the edge of Cowms Moor. Cross a stile and keep a stone wall on your right as you begin descending to Hayridge Farm. Walk through the farm and turn left and follow the road towards Alport Farm, where there is a camping barn. However, you only follow the road for 175 yards before turning right on the path through the trees to Alport Bridge. Cross the A57 road and follow the track down to the River Ashop, where there is a ford and footbridge. Contine ahead on the track to open country. Here turn left along the track, which soon descends to the River Ashop and Rowlee Bridge. Cross the bridge and ascend the now tarmaced lane to the A57 once more. Cross over and ascend past Rowlee Farm and follow the zig-zag track beyond. After ¼ mile the track levels off and you pass Bellhagg Barn on your right. ¼ mile later you reach a crossroads of paths. Turn right and descend and in ten minutes reach the drive on your right for Hagg Farm.

KINDER DOWNFALL

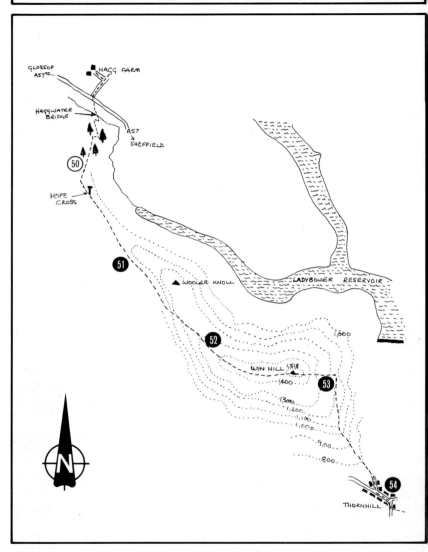

WIN HILL — According to tradition a battle was fought in the valley below along the banks of the River Noe in the 7th century. The winners camped the night before on Win Hill and the losers on Lose Hill.

HAGG FARM TO HATHERSAGE — 8 MILES

**MAPS — O.S. 1:25,000 Outdoor Leisure Map — The Dark Peak.
- O.S. 1:25,000 Pathfinder Series Sheet No SK28/38 — Sheffield.**

WALKING INSTRUCTIONS

Descend the Hostel drive to the A57 road. Cross and continue descending to the bridge over the River Ashop — Haggwater Bridge. On the other side turn right and follow the ascending path through the trees, which after a few yards turns left. After ¼ mile turn right and left shortly afterwards as you ascend along a well-defined path in the trees. Emerging from the trees, continue ahead a short distance before turning left towards Hope Cross. Follow the path from the Cross — now the line of a Roman road — for the next mile. Where it descends towards Fullwood Stile Farm, turn left and keep to the high ground, still on a path, and now heading for the summit of Win Hill 1½ miles away.

The rocky summit of the hill provides extensive views over much of the area through which you have walked. Descend the hill, heading due east. After crossing the ladder stile, descend through Winhill Plantation. Approximately ¼ mile from the stile you reach the wall of another plantation; here you turn right along the distinct path. For the next ½ mile you contour round the slopes of Win Hill before turning left and ascending the ridge to Thornhill village ¾ mile away.

LADY BOWER RESERVOIR FROM WIN HILL

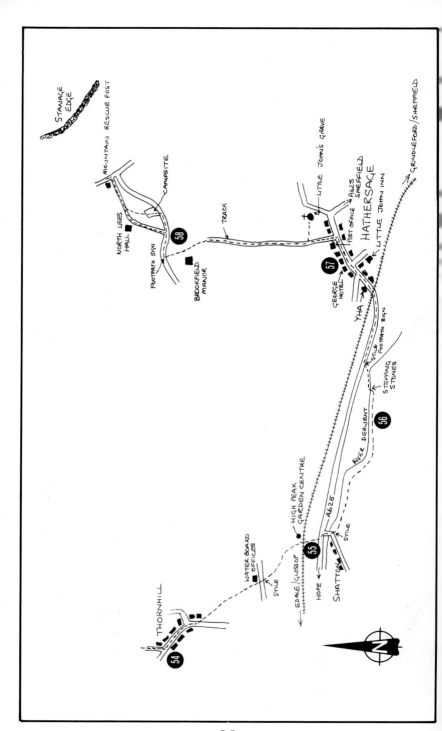

STANAGE EDGE

MOUNTAIN RESCUE POST

CAMPSITE

NORTH LEES HALL

TRACK

FOOTPATH SIGN

58

BROOKFIELD MANOR

LITTLE JOHN'S GRAVE

POST OFFICE   A625 SHEFFIELD

HATHERSAGE

LITTLE JOHN INN

57

GEORGE HOTEL

YHA

TO GRINDLEFORD/SHEFFIELD

STILE   FOOTPATH SIGN

STILE

STEPPING STONES

RIVER DERWENT

56

HIGH PEAK GARDEN CENTRE

A625

STILE

WATER BOARD OFFICES

55

EDALE/GLOSSOP

HOPE

SHATTON

STILE

THORNHILL

STILE

54

N

24

In the village turn left and right shortly afterwards on Thornhill Lane. Almost immediately, and on the righthand side of the last house on your left, turn left through the stile and follow the curving path around the edge of the field to the railway line. Once through the stile turn right and walk through the railway bridge to the A625 road beyond. On your left is the car park of High Peak Garden Centre. Cross the A625 road and follow the Shatton road. Just over the bridge over the river, turn left through the stile and follow the path along the righthand bank of the Derwent River for the next 1½ miles. Upon reaching the curving stepping stones across the river, turn
left and cross the steps. On the other side follow the path along the bankside and up to the A625 road. Turn right and walk beside the road into Hathersage, passing the Youth Hostel on your left.

Continue up the main street of Hathersage to the Post Office on your left. Turn left here along the lane, and at the end turn left along the rough track (Baulk Lane). A short distance along here on your right is the path to Hathersage Church. Continue along the track and follow it for almost a mile. As you near Brookfield Manor, and as directed by path signs, turn left and follow the path along the righthand side of the buildings. At the minor road beyond, turn right and walk along the road past the entrance to North Lees Hall. Shortly afterwards you reach the entrance to the campsite.

HATHERSAGE — Hathersage is extremely rich in local and national history. Many old buildings and industries remain. In the 19th century the village had a thriving needle manufacturing trade and several of the old works are still standing. Just behind the Hathersage Inn in Besom Lane is a three-storey high building built by the Furniss family in 1781 and used to manufacture buttons. In the churchyard is the grave to Little John, the faithful companion of Robin Hood. From a 29½ inch thigh bone taken from the grave, Little John would have been eight foot tall. The 14th century church contains several brasses to the Eyre family who once owned more than 20,000 acres in the area. North Lees Hall was built by the Eyre family as were several others in the surrounding area.

NORTH LEES HALL — Elizabethan turreted building built by the Eyre family in about 1594. The nearby Moorseats Hall has Bronte connections for Charlotte Bronte stayed here, resulting in her famous novel, Jane Eyre. In the book Moorseats is known as Moor House and North Lees Hall is described as Marsh End.

HATHERSAGE TO ROBIN HOOD INN — 13 MILES

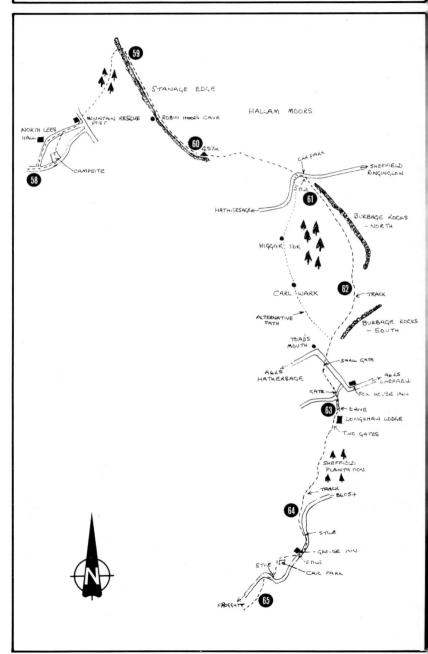

STANAGE EDGE

HALLAM MOORS

MOUNTAIN RESCUE POST

ROBIN HOOD'S CAVE

NORTH LEES HALL

CAMPSITE

58

59

60 457m

CAR PARK

→ SHEFFIELD RINGINGLOW

STILE

HATHERSAGE →

61

BURBAGE ROCKS – NORTH

HIGGAR TOR

CARL WARK

62 TRACK

ALTERNATIVE PATH

BURBAGE ROCKS – SOUTH

TOADS MOUTH

SMALL GATE

A625 HATHERSAGE

A625 SHEFFIELD

FOX HOUSE INN

GATE

63 ← DRIVE

LONGSHAW LODGE

TWO GATES

SHEFFIELD PLANTATION

TRACK

B6054

64

STILE

GROUSE INN

STILE

STILE

CAR PARK

FROGGATT

65

N

HATHERSAGE TO ROBIN HOOD'S INN —
13 MILES

**MAPS — O.S. 1:25,000 Pathfinder Series Sheet No SK28/38 —
Sheffield.
- O.S. 1:25,000 Outdoor Leisure Map — The White Peak — East
Sheet.**

WALKING INSTRUCTIONS

At the top end of the campsite is a signposted path for Stanage. If you stayed in
Hathersage there is no need to walk to the campsite — you can walk up the road to
North Lees Hall and join the path from the campsite. Ascend to the road beneath
Stanage Edge, close to the Mountain Rescue building. Cross the road and follow
the well-used path up onto the summit of Stanage Edge. Turn right and walk along
the top for the next mile to the triangulation pillar. The path curves to your left
before descending to the road close to Burbage Brook. Turn left, and the other side
of the car park is the start of the wide track down the Burbage Valley. For the next
1½ miles you descend gradually along the valley.

As you walk along, on your right is Higgar Tor and Carl Wark — you can walk over
these as an alternative route bearing left after Carl Wark to the track end. At the
end of the track, cross the A625 road to the stile and continue on another path
which soon curves left onto another track which you follow to the road opposite the
entrance to Longshaw Lodge. Cross the B6521 road and walk along the drive
towards the Lodge. Just before the buildings turn right and follow the path beneath
the lawn to a gate. Go through this and the subsequent one, and follow the wide
track through Longshaw Estate for the next 1½ miles. Upon reaching the B6054
road turn right, and just past the Grouse Inn, 200 yards later, turn right and cross the
field. In the trees turn left (there is a car park here on your left) and follow the path to
a small stream and up to the B6054 road. Cross this to the stile and another track on
your left. This will lead you along the next gritstone edges — Froggatt and Curbar.

HIGGAR TOR — A huge leaning block 45 ft. high, upon which are some of the
most testing rock climbs in the area.

CARL WARK — A former Iron Age fort and a large wall and boundary wall are
still visible today.

LONGSHAW — A former shooting lodge and estate of the Duke of Rutland.
Now owned by the National Trust, who have an Information Centre here and Tea
Room.

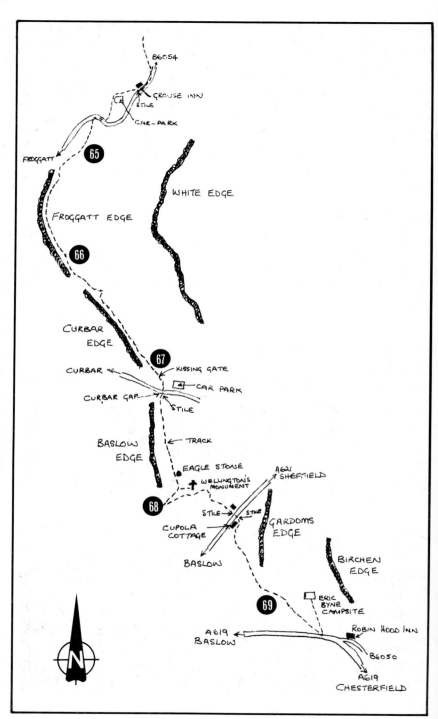

After 2½ miles you descend to the road at Curbar Gap. Turn left then right onto another track and follow this along the moor on the left of Baslow Edge. After almost a mile you pass Eagle Tor on your left before reaching Wellington's Monument. Turn right here, and after 250 yards turn left and descend beneath the monument. After 250 yards the path turns sharp right as you descend to a stile, bridge and A621 road. Cross this, and on the left of Cupola Cottage is the stile and path for Gardoms Edge. Follow this gently-ascending path to your right, aiming for the righthand edge of the rocks. Continue along the path, gradually descending to the A619. Turn left and left again for the Robin Hood Inn, where permission to camp at the Eric Byne Memorial campsite can be obtained. You will have noticed the sign and drive for this site on your left. The campsite is admirably placed with Birchen Edge close by.

GRITSTONE EDGES — Running along the eastern side of the Peak District is a whole string of 'edges' rising up to 120 ft. high. Here rock climbing became established, and all the edges have hundreds of routes of varying difficulty — Stanage alone has over 600! The edges were, in the 18th and 19th Centuries, the workground for the manufacture of millstones. A look along some of the edges, such as the southern end of Burbage or on Froggatt, will reveal many discarded stones.

EAGLE STONE

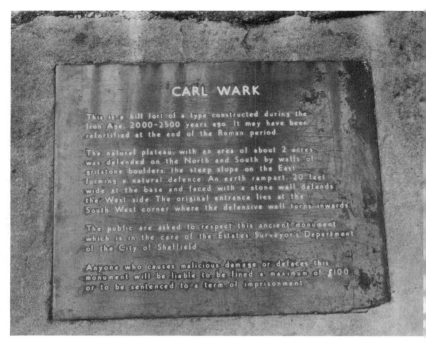

CARL WARK PLAQUE

CARL WARK

CHATSWORTH HOUSE

PEAKLAND WAY WALKERS AT QUEEN MARY'S BOWER

ROBIN HOOD INN TO BIRCHOVER — 10 MILES

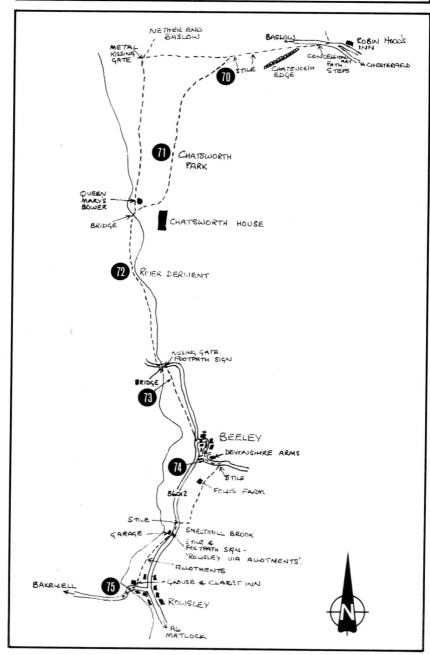

ROBIN HOOD'S INN TO BIRCHOVER — 10 MILES

MAPS — O.S. 1:25,000 Outdoor Leisure Map — The White Peak — East Sheet.

WALKING INSTRUCTIONS

A short easy day allowing ample time to explore Chatsworth Park and House. Just down the A619 road from the Inn towards Baslow is the concessionary footpath and sign on the lefthand side of the road. Descend the steps and cross the brook via the wooden bridge. Turn right and follow the track first beneath Chatsworth Edge and then onto Chatsworth Park, reached via two exceptionally high stiles. Once in the Park and as signposted, you have a choice of routes — either keep straight ahead and aim for Baslow and its shops or turn left and head direct to Chatsworth House. After approximately one and a half miles across the open grassland you will reach the House and Queen Mary's Bower.

Cross the bridge over the River Derwent and walk along the riverside for just over a mile to the road and another bridge over the river. Here turn left and cross the bridge before turning right, as footpath signposted, and cross the field to Beeley, reaching the road opposite the church. Cross the road B6012 and walk up past the church on your left. Turn right and descend the road to the Devonshire Arms. Walk up the road on the right of the Inn and, after 150 yards, turn right, as footpath signed and stiled, and follow the well-stiled path across eight fields, keeping Folds Farm on your right. After the eighth field you descend through the trees towards Smeltingmill Brook. Here the path turns right to a stile and the B6012 road.

Turn left, and just past a garage on your right turn right, as footpath signposted — "Allotments to Rowsley". First you walk close to the River Derwent before the allotments and emerge in Rowsley via the side of the Grouse and Claret Inn. Turn right along the A6 road and just round the corner turn left along School Lane. Follow this road across the River Wye and close to the river for a quarter of a mile to a lefthand bend, where on the right is the stile and footpath sign. First you ascend as you curve round the slope before descending to a small plantation. A short ascent from here brings you to the lefthand side of Dove House Farm. Turn right at the road and descend for a quarter of a mile to the stile and path sign — "Stanton in Peak ¾ mile". After the first field you begin ascending through the fields and above Smithy Wood. If in doubt of the route the spire of Stanton Church acts as your guide. You reach the village opposite the church.

CHATSWORTH HOUSE — The most famous house in the Peak District and one of the masterpieces of Britain. The present building is still lived in by the Dukes of Devonshire, whose predecessors built the house and estate. The gardens are extensive, and the house is overflowing with treasures. A few hours spent here is very worthwhile.

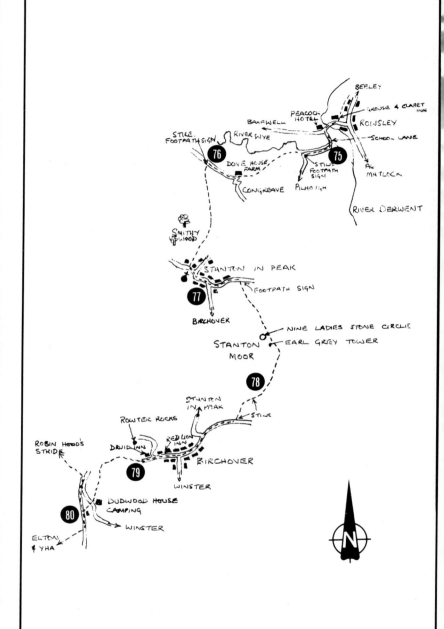

BEELEY

GROUSE & CLARET INN

PEACOCK HOTEL

BAKEWELL

ROWSLEY

STILE
FOOTPATH SIGN

RIVER WYE

SCHOOL LANE

76

DOVE HOUSE FARM

75

STILE FOOTPATH SIGN

A6 MATLOCK

CONGREAVE

PILHOUGH

RIVER DERWENT

SMITHY WOOD

STANTON IN PEAK

FOOTPATH SIGN

77

BIRCHOVER

NINE LADIES STONE CIRCLE

STANTON MOOR

EARL GREY TOWER

78

STANTON IN PEAK

ROWTER ROCKS

STILE

ROBIN HOOD'S STRIDE

DRUID INN

RED LION INN

79

BIRCHOVER

WINSTER

80

DUDWOOD HOUSE CAMPING

ELTON & YHA

WINSTER

N

Turn left and continue ascending now out of the village. Take the second road on your left, through the trees and quarry remains. At the top turn right as signposted and follow the well-trodden path on Stanton Moor. Keep to the lefthand edge of the heatherclad moorland, as this will bring you to the Earl Grey Tower and spectacular views over the Derwent Valley to Matlock. One and a half miles around the moorland brings you to a minor road. Turn right and follow this past the quarries on your right and descend into Birchover village. At the end of the main street, at the Druid Inn, keep straight ahead and descend the narrow lane past a small chapel on your left. At the bottom continue on a track, and where it turns sharp left keep straight ahead on a grass track to a stile. Continue ahead with the wall on your right, and after 200 yards the path curves due north and you descend the field to the stile at Dudwood House and the campsite. Elton Youth Hostel is a mile away.

ROWSLEY — The Peacock Inn was built in 1652 as a private residence for the "man of affairs" to Lady Manners, the mother of the 8th Duke of Rutland. It was she who founded Lady Manners School in Bakewell, which still exists today.

STANTON MOOR — Rich in archaeological remains. The Nine Ladies Stone Circle dates from the Bronze Age and many mounds have been found used by the Beaker folk. The Earl Grey Tower was built in 1832.

BIRCHOVER — Behind the Druid Inn are Rowter Rocks, which have stone seats, passageways, rooms and steps carved 270 years ago. There are also two rocking stones. The small chapel dates from the 18th Century and has a monument to Joan Waste in the porch. She was burnt to death as a heretic in the Windmill Pit in Derby in 1556.

EARL GREY TOWER, STANTON MOOR

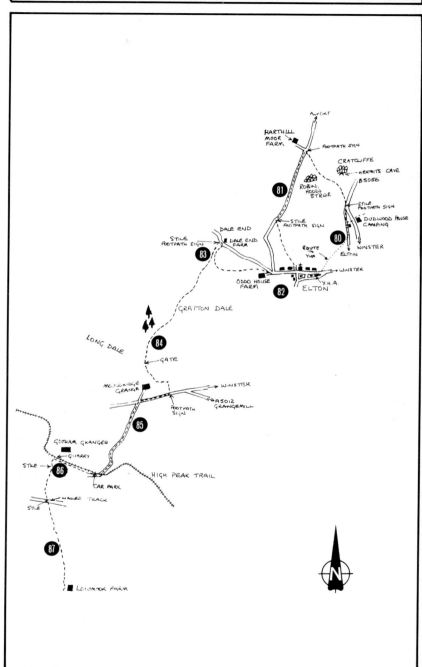

BIRCHOVER TO ASHBOURNE — 15 MILES

MAPS — O.S. 1:25,000 Outdoor Leisure Map — The White Peak — East and West sheets.
- O.S. 1:25,000 Pathfinder Series Sheet No SK04/14 — Ashbourne and the Churnet Valley.

WALKING INSTRUCTIONS

The final section, and one of the most beautiful. Cross the B5056 road at the entrance to Dudwood House to the stile opposite, and follow the path across the field to the righthand side of the house. At the minor road here turn right, and 200 yards later turn left via the stile and footpath sign and ascend the track towards Robin Hood's Stride. Keep the field boundary on your immediate left as you ascend. At the top the rocks are on your left. Keep straight ahead to a stile and cross two fields to the road opposite the entrance to Harthill Moor Farm. Turn left and walk along the road which gradually ascends for a while. After descending a short distance, and ³/₄ mile along the road, you reach a stile and path sign on your left. Descend the field before ascending to Elton, entering the village close to its church.

At the main road turn right and walk through the village for the next ¹/₄ mile, and most of the time you are gradually descending. At the entrance to Oddo House Farm turn left then right and walk around the farm buildings. Keep straight ahead, and the stiles will guide you through the fields and down to a shallow dale. Turn right here and descend to Dale End and Farm. Turn left at the road and left again almost immediately, close to the telephone kiosk and as footpath signposted. You are now back in limestone country as you walk along the floor of Gratton Dale. The early part of the dale can be very muddy. You walk along the dale for the next one and three quarter miles. After passing a small plantation on your right and walking through numerous dolomitic limestone boulders, you reach a gate. Here turn left and begin ascending out of the dale to a stone wall which you walk round, keeping it on your right all the time, to reach the A5012 road.

Turn right and walk along the road to the entrance to Mouldridge Grange on your right. Here turn left along the minor road signposted for Parwich, which is your destination as well. You follow this road for the next mile to the car park on the High Peak Trail. Leave the road here and follow the trail to your right. After a third of a mile you pass a very small quarry on your left. Leave the trail via the path on the right of the rocks and ascend to the stile. The next three miles to Parwich are along a little-used path, but it is well stiled all the way as you head almost due south. First you pass between the Gotham and Chapel Plantation before angling to your right to the end of the Gotham Plantation. Beyond you cross a walled track before crossing subsequent fields to Lowmoor Plantation and Farm. Walk around the farm's righthand side via path and stile. You then ascend steeply before crossing four further fields to a minor road near Hilltop Farm. Cross the road via stiles and follow the footpath-signed path towards Parwich. You keep straight ahead for three fields before bearing right and descending into Parwich village.

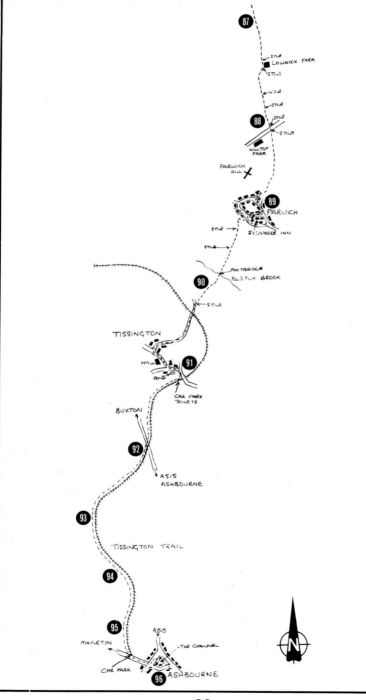

87

STILE
LOWMOOR FARM
STILE

STILE
STILE
88 STILE
STILE
HILLTOP FARM

PARWICH HILL ✗

89
PARWICH

SYCAMORE INN

STILE
STILE

90
FOOTBRIDGE
FLETCH BROOK

STILE

TISSINGTON

HALL
POND
91

CAR PARK TOILETS

BUXTON

92

A515 ASHBOURNE

93

TISSINGTON TRAIL

94

95
A515
THE CHANNEL
MAPLETON
CAR PARK
96 ASHBOURNE

N

After a final drink in the Sycamore Inn, turn right then left into the fields and follow the Tissington path. First you skirt the southern end of the village for 150 yards before turning left and ascending in a south-westerly direction. After the fourth field you descend to the Bletch Brook, which you cross via a footbridge. Ascend the three fields beyond to the track and bridge over the Tissington Trail. Turn left and cross the bridge and continue on this tarmaced road to the main street in Tissington village, 1/2 mile away. Turn left and walk down the road, passing the Hall on your right and Church on your left. At the bottom turn left past the village pond on your right, before turning right down the road into Tissington Car Park and Trail. Turn right and walk along the Trail for the next four miles to Ashbourne. At the end of the Trail turn right then left up the road. At the top — North Avenue — turn left and then right down The Channel back to the Market Place and Cross — journey's end!

ROBIN HOOD'S STRIDE — Gritstone outcrop whose distance between the twin towers is said to be the length of Robin Hood's stride. The nearby and much higher Cratcliffe Tor has a hermit's cave at its base with carved crucifix, made in the 14th Century.

HIGH PEAK TRAIL — A former railway line that extended 33 miles, linking the Cromford Canal near Matlock with the Peak Forest Canal at Whaley Bridge. The railway was unique with nine inclines up which the trains were hauled. 17 miles of the line were converted to a pedestrian way in the early 1970s.

PARWICH — Attractive limestone village whose church was rebuilt last century. Parts of the earlier building are incorporated into it, including a Norman tympanum.

TISSINGTON VILLAGE — The prettiest village in the Peak District, renowned for its annual well-dressing ceremony that takes place here in late May. The Hall dates from 1608 and was built by the Fitzherbert family, who still reside here today. The church, which dates back to Norman times, has several impressive monuments to the Fitzherberts.

ROBIN HOOD'S STRIDE

AMENITIES GUIDE

VILLAGE	B&B	YHA	CAMP	INN	CAFE	SHOP	P.O.	TRANSPORT
ASHBOURNE	*		*	*	*	*	*	*
MAPLETON				*		*		
ILAM HALL		*						
WETTONMILL			*			*		
HULME END	*		*	*		*	*	
LONGNOR	*			*	*	*	*	*
EARL STERNDALE				*				
BLACKWELL			*					
PEAK FOREST	*			*	*	*		
ROWTER FARM			*					
BARBER BOOTH	*		*			*		
SNAKE ROAD		*		*	*			
HAGG FARM		*	*			*		
HATHERSAGE	*	*	*	*	*	*	*	*
LONGSHAW				*	*	*		*
ROBIN HOOD			*	*				
BASLOW	*			*	*	*	*	*
BEELEY	*			*	*	*	*	*
ROWSLEY	*			*	*	*	*	*
STANTON IN PEAK				*		*	*	*
BIRCHOVER	*		*	*	*	*	*	*
ELTON		*		*				
PARWICH				*				

GROUSE INN

LIST OF INNS

ASHBOURNE —	Coach & Horses Green Man Hotel Plough Inn Wheel Inn
HULME END —	Manifold Valley Hotel
LONGNOR —	Cheshire Cheese Crewe & Harpur Arms
EARL STERNDALE —	The Quiet Woman
PEAK FOREST —	The Devonshire Arms
EDALE —	Old Nag's Head Rambler Inn
SNAKE PASS —	Snake Inn
HATHERSAGE —	Little John Inn Hathersage Inn George Hotel
LONGSHAW —	Fox House Inn Grouse Inn
BIRCHEN EDGE —	Robin Hood's Inn
BASLOW —	Devonshire Arms
BEELEY —	Devonshire Arms
ROWSLEY —	Grouse and Claret Inn
STANTON IN PEAK —	The Flying Childers
BIRCHOVER —	The Druid Inn Red Lion Inn
PARWICH —	The Sycamore Inn

BED AND BREAKFAST GUIDE —
A random selection. Many more are found open during the summer months.

ASHBOURNE —

Mrs. A. Sansum, The Vicarage, 61 Belle Vue Rd.
Tel. Ashbourne 43129

The Clifton Hotel, Station Road.
Tel. Ashbourne 3330

THORPE —

Mrs. Challinor, The Old Orchard, Stoney Lane.
Tel. Thorpe Cloud 410

Mrs. F.M. Gould, St. Leonard's Cottage.
Tel. Thorpe Cloud 224

HARTINGTON —

Mrs. B. Blackburn, Bank House, Market Place.
Tel. Hartington 465

LITTON —

Mrs. H. Radford, Hall Farm House.
Tel. Tideswell 871124

PEAK FOREST —

Devonshire Arms.
Tel. Buxton 3875

CASTLETON —

Mrs. P. Fowler, Burrows House.
Tel. Hope Valley 20253

Mrs. S. Petford, Ramblers Rest, Millbridge.
Tel. Hope Valley 20125

EDALE —

J.E. Chapman, Barber Booth.
Tel. Hope Valley 70227

Rambler Inn.
Tel. Hope Valley 70268

BAMFORD —

Mrs. J.M. Oldfield, Meadows Reach, 12 Main Rd.
Tel. Hope Valley 51216

HATHERSAGE —

Mrs. R. Mellors, Elmhirst, Ninelands Road.
Tel. Hope Valley 50695

CURBAR —

Mrs. G. Willis, Windrush, Riddings Lane.
Tel. Hope Valley 30201

PILSLEY —

Devonshire Arms.
Tel. Baslow 3258

BIRCHOVER —   Mrs. C. Hobbs, Brickfields Cottage, Eagle Tor.
                     Tel. Winster 459

ALDWARK —-   Mrs. D. Forsey, Tithe Farm.
                     Tel. Carsington 263

YOUTH   HOSTELS —
on or close to the route.

ILAM —   Ilam Hall, Ashbourne, Derbyshire, DE6 2AZ.
                     Tel. Thorpe Cloud (033529) 212

HARTINGTON —   (2 miles off route)
                     Hartington Hall, Hartington, Buxton, Derbyshire,
                     SK17 0AT
                     Tel. Hartington (029884) 223

BUXTON —   (4 miles off route)
                     Sherbrook Lodge, Harpur Hill Road, Buxton,
                     Derbyshire, SK17 9NB.
                     Tel. Buxton (0298) 2287

CASTLETON —   (1 mile off route)
                     Castleton Hall, Castleton, Sheffield, S30 2WG.
                     Tel. Hope Valley (0433) 20235

EDALE —   (1.5 miles off route)
                     Rowland Cote, Nether Booth, Edale, Sheffield,
                     S30 2ZH
                     Tel. Hope Valley (0433) 70302

HAGG FARM —   Snake Road, Bamford, Sheffield, S30 2BJ.
                     Tel. Hope Valley (0433) 51594

HATHERSAGE —   Youth Hostel, Castleton Road, Hathersage,
                     Sheffield, S30 1AH.
                     Tel. Hope Valley (0433) 50493

BAKEWELL —   Fly Hill, Bakewell, Derbyshire, DE4 1DN
                     Tel. Bakewell (062981) 2313
                     (4 miles off route)

ELTON —   Elton Old Hall, Main Street, Elton, Matlock,
                     Derbyshire, DE4 2BW
                     Tel. Winster (062988) 394

CAMPING SITES —
on or within 2 miles of the route.

ASHBOURNE —   Sandybrook Hall
                       G.R. SK 182482
                       Tel. Ashbourne 42679

ILAM —   Garden Farm, Ilam Moor Lane.
                       G.R. SK 132513
                       Tel. Thorpe Cloud 473

WETTON MILL —   Wetton, Nr. Ashbourne.
                       G.R. SK 095560

BLACKWELL —   Cottage Farm
                       G.R. SK 125721
                       Tel. Taddington 330

CASTLETON —   Rowter Farm
                       G.R. SK 132822

EDALE —   Waterside Farm
                       G.R. SK 118848
                       Tel. Hope Valley 70215

                       Fieldhead Campsite
                       G.R. SK 124856
                       Tel. Hope Valley 70216

                       Upper Booth Farm
                       G.R. SK 103855
                       Tel. Hope Valley 70250

ASHOPTON —   Hagg Farm
                       G.R. SK 161889
                       Tel. Hope Valley 51594

HATHERSAGE —   North Lees Campsite, Birley Lane.
                       G.R. SK 235832
                       Tel. Hope Valley 50838

BASLOW —   Eric Byne Memorial Campsite, Birchen Edge.
                       G.R. SK 278723

BIRCHOVER —   Barn Farm
                       G.R. SK 242623
                       Tel. Winster 245

                       Dudwood House, Nr. Winster.
                       G.R. SK 231617

CAMPING BARNS —

ALPORT CASTLE —   G.R. SK 135910
This is a camping barn — no tent needed!
Bookings to Peak National Park Study Centre,
Losehill Hall, Castleton, Derbyshire, S30 2WB.

SNAKE INN —   Camping Barn adjacent to the inn.

Random lists of the more common birds and flow ers to be seen en route:-

BIRDS

Limestone country -

Tree-creeper
Blue Tit
Curlew
Coot
Grey Wagtail
Lapwing
Little Owl
Redstart
Hawfinch
Swallow
Yellowhammer
Wren
Wheatear
Moorhen
Dipper
Raven
Tufted Duck
Robin
Bullfinch
Redpoll
Whitethroat
Lesser Black-Backed Gull
Nuthatch
Great Tit

Kingfisher
Blackbird
Mallard
Fieldfare
Marsh Tits
Sedge Warbler
Wood Pigeon
Pied Wagtail

Moorland country -

Red Grouse
Wheatear
Dunlin
Ring Ouzel
Golden Plover
Twite
Meadow Pipit
Curlew
Skylark

Gritstone country -

Tree-creeper
Whinchat
Sparrow-hawk
Wheatear
Blue Tit
Grey Heron
Magpie
Skylark
Blackbird
Pheasant
Mistle Thrush
Great Spotted Woodpecker
Starling
Bullfinch
Ring Ouzel
Wren
Great Tit

Robin
Greenfinch
Moorhen
Rook
Wood Pigeon
Song Thrush
Chaffinch
Common Sandpiper
Crow
Meadow Pipit
Curlew
Long Tailed Tit
Linnet
Coot
Cuckoo
Black Headed Gull
House Sparrow

FLOWERS

Limestone country -

Meadow Cranesbill
Primrose
Wood Anemone
Wood Sage
Globe Flower
Musk Thistle
Crosswort
Lesser Meadow Rue
Bluebell
Ramsons
Mountain Melick
Butterbur
Herb Robert
Wood Forget-Me-Not
Thyme
Bloody Cranesbill
Dog's Mercury
Lily of the Valley
Arum
Wood Sorrel
Ground Ivy
Marjoram
Harebell
Rough Hawkbit

Mossy Saxifrage
Kidney Vetch
Devil's Bit Scabious
Carline Thistle
Grass of Parnassus
Early Purple Orchid
Monkey Flower
Hart's Tongue Fern
White Dead Nettle
Rosebay Willow-Herb
Knapweed
Red Campion
Marsh Marigold
Clover
Goatsbeard
Dog Rose
Greater Burnet Saxifrage
Clustered Bell Flower
Small Scabious
Slender Bedstraw
Eyebright
Hawkweed Oxtongue
Birdsfoot Trefoil
Germander Speedwell

Scurvygrass
Twayblade
Yellow Archangel
Meadow Buttercup
Watercress
Blackthorn
Foxglove
Yellow Stonecrop
Bugle
Limestone Fern
Sheep's Fescue
Rock Rose
Milkwort
Cowslip

Jacob's Ladder
Mountain Pansies
Male Fern
Coltsfoot
Ragged Robin
Lady's Smock
Gorse
Lesser Celandine
Ox-eye Daisy
Stitchwort
Rattle
Tufted Vetch
Nettle-leaved Bell Flower
Great Hairy Willow-Herb

Moorland -

Ling
Cranberry
Butterwort
Maidenhair Spleenwort Fern
Bilberry
Crowberry

Sphagnum Moss
Cowberry
Bog Asphodel
Cotton Grass
Round-leaved Sundew

Gritstone country -

Bilberry
Eyebright
Devil's Bit Scabious
Tormentil
Common Bent
Meadowsweet
Heath Bedstraw
Periwinkle
Poppy
Honesty
Ling
Bluebell
Sheep's Sorrel
Sheep's Fescue
Marsh Thistle

Purple Moor-grass
Gorse
Lesser Celandine
Foxglove
Snowberry
Wood Sorrel
Hard Fern
Wavy Hair Grass
Sneezewort
Mat Grass
Policeman's Helmet
Red Campion
Marsh Marigold
Clover
Yellow Loosestrife

LOG

DATE STARTED:-------------- DATE COMPLETED------------------

ROUTE POINT	MILE NO.	COMMENTS
ASHBOURNE	0	
MAPLETON	$1\frac{1}{4}$	
COLDWALL BRIDGE	$3\frac{1}{4}$	
ILAM HALL	5	
THROWLEY HALL	7	
BEESTON TOR	8	
THORS CAVE	9	
WETTONMILL	10	
HULME END	$12\frac{1}{2}$	
BRUND MILL	14	
LONGNOR	16	
RIVER DOVE	17	
EARL STERNDALE	18	
QUARRY	19	
DEEP DALE	21	
TOPLEY PIKE	22	
CHEE DALE	23	
BLACKWELL	24	
WORMHILL	25	
PETER DALE	27	
PEAK FOREST	$29\frac{1}{2}$	
BROCTOR	30	
OLD MOOR	31	
ROWTOR FARM	32	
MAM TOR	33	
HOLLINS CROSS	34	
BARBER BOOTH	$35\frac{1}{2}$	
UPPER BOOTH	$36\frac{1}{2}$	
JACOB'S LADDER	38	
KINDER LOW	39	
KINDER DOWNFALL	40	
ASHOP HEAD	42	
SNAKE ROAD	$44\frac{1}{2}$	
OYSTER CLOUGH	46	
ALPORT BRIDGE	$47\frac{1}{2}$	
HAGG FARM	$49\frac{1}{2}$	

HOPE CROSS	50½	
WIN HILL	53	
THORNHILL	54	
SHATTON	55	
STEPPING STONES	56	
HATHERSAGE	57	
NORTH LEES CAMPSITE	58	
STANAGE EDGE	59	
BURBAGE VALLEY	61	
FOX HOUSE INN	63	
B6054 ROAD	65	
FROGGATT EDGE	66	
CURBAR GAP	67	
WELLINGTON'S MONUMENT	68	
ROBIN HOOD INN	69½	
CHATSWORTH PARK	71	
BEELEY	74	
ROWSLEY	75	
CONGREAVE ROAD	76	
STANTON IN PEAK	77	
STANTON MOOR	78	
BIRCHOVER	79	
DUDWOOD HOUSE	80	
ELTON	82	
DALE END	83	
GRATTON DALE	84	
MOULDRIDGE GRANGE	85	
HIGH PEAK TRAIL	86	
LOWMOOR FARM	87½	
PARWICH	89	
BLETCH BROOK	90	
TISSINGTON	91	
TISSINGTON TRAIL	93	
ASHBOURNE	96	

TRAIL PROFILE

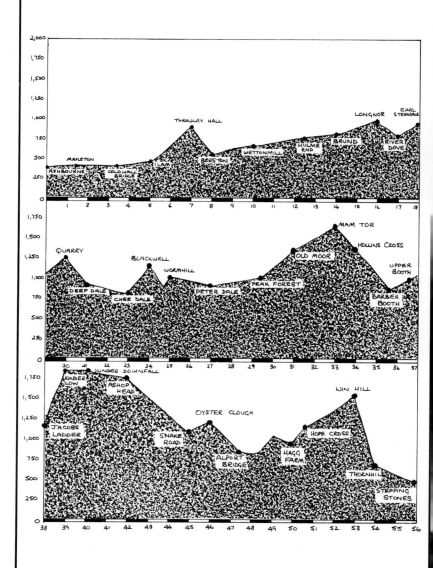

TRAIL PROFILE

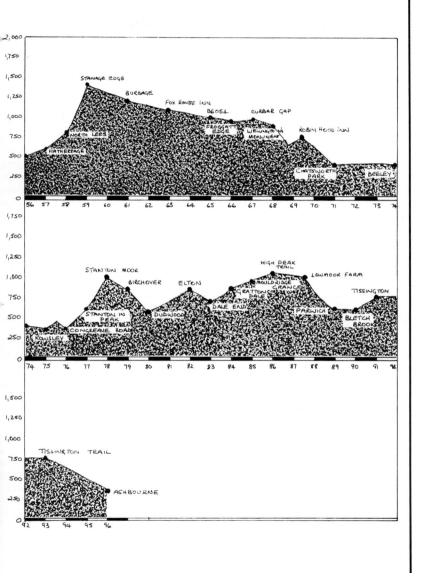

EQUIPMENT NOTES — some personal thoughts

BOOTS — preferably with a full leather upper, of mediu weight, with a vibram sole. I always add a foam cushioned insole to help cushion the base of my feet.

SOCKS — I generally wear two thick pairs as this helps minimise blisters. The inner pair are of loop stitch variety and approximately 80% wool. The outer are a thick rib pair of approximately 80% wool.

WATERPROOFS — for general walking I wear a T shirt or shirt with a cotton wind jacket on top. You generate heat as you walk and I prefer to layer my clothes to avoid getting too hot. Depending on the season will dictate how many layers you wear. In soft rain I just use my wind jacket for I know it quickly dries out. In heavy downpours I slip on a neoprene lined cagoule, and although hot and clammy it does keep me reasonably dry. Only in extreme conditions will I don overtrousers, much preferring to get wet and feel comfortable.

FOOD — as I walk I carry bars of chocolate, for they provide instant energy and are light to carry. In winter a flask of hot coffee is welcome. I never carry water and find no hardship from doing so, but this is a personal matter! From experience I find the more I drink the more I want and sweat. You should always carry some extra food such as Kendal mint cake, for emergencies.

RUCKSACKS — for day walking I use a climbing rucksac of about 40 litre capacity and although it leaves excess space it does mean that the sac is well padded, with an internal frame and padded shoulder straps. Inside apart from the basics for the day I carry gloves, balaclava, spare pullover and a pair of socks.

MAP & COMPASS — when I am walking I always have the relevant map — preferably the 1:25,000 scale — open in my hand. This enables me to constantly check that I am walking the right way. In case of bad weather I carry a compass, which once mastered gives you complete confidence in thick cloud or mist.

REMEMBER AND OBSERVE THE COUNTRY CODE

Enjoy the countryside and respect its life and work.

Guard against all risk of fire.

Fasten all gates.

Keep your dogs under close control.

Keep to public paths across farmland.

Use gates and stiles to cross fences, hedges and walls.

Leave livestock, crops and machinery alone.

Take your litter home — pack it in, pack it out.

Help to keep all water clean.

Protect wildlife, plants and trees.

Take special care on country roads.

Make no unnecessary noise.

THE HIKER'S CODE

Hike only along marked routes — do not leave the trail.

Use stiles to climb fences; close gates.

Camp only in designated campsites.

Carry a light-weight stove.

Leave the Trail cleaner than you found it.

Leave flowers and plants for others to enjoy.

Keep dogs on a leash.

Protect and do not disturb wildlife.

Use the trail at your own risk.

Leave only your thanks — take nothing but photographs.

OTHER CHALLENGE WALKS BY JOHN N MERRILL -

DAY CHALLENGES -

John Merrill's White Peak Challenge Walk — 25 miles.
Circular walk from Bakewell involving 3,600 feet of ascent.

John Merrill's Dark Peak Challenge Walk — 24 miles.
Circular walk from Hathersage involving 3,300 feet of ascent.

John Merrill's Staffordshire Moorlands Challenge Walk — 2 miles.
Circular walk from Oakamoor involving 2,200 feet of ascent.

John Merrill"s Yorkshire Dales Challenge Walk — 23 miles.
Circular walk from Kettlewell involving 3,600 feet of ascent.

John Merrill's North Yorkshire Moors Challenge Walk — 2 miles.
Circular walk from Goathland — a seaside bash — involvin 2,000 feet of ascent.

The Little John Challenge Walk — 28 miles.
Circular walk from Edwinstowe in Sherwood Forest — Robi Hood country.

Peak District End to End Walks.
1. Gritstone Edge Walk — 23 miles down the eastern edg system.
2. Limestone Dale Walk — 24 miles down the limestone dale from Buxton to Ashbourne.

Forthcoming titles —

John Merrill's Snowdonia Challenge Walk.

The Rutland Water Challenge Walk.

MULTIPLE DAY CHALLENGE WALKS -

The Limey Way — 40 miles
Down twenty limestone dales from Castleton to Thorpe in th Peak District.

The River's Way — 43 miles.
Down the five main river systems of the Peak District, from Edal the end of the Pennine Way, to Ilam.

Peak District High Level Route — 90 miles
Circular walk from Matlock taking in the highest and remotest parts of the Peak District.

COASTAL WALKS —

The Isle of Wight Coast Path — 77 miles.
Complete encirclement of a magnificent island.

Forthcoming books -

The Cleveland Way

The Pembrokeshire Coast Path.

DESCENDING TO HAYRIDGE FARM

TISSINGTON HALL

OTHER BOOKS BY JOHN N. MERRILL PUBLISHED BY JNM PUBLICATIONS

DAY WALK GUIDES -

SHORT CIRCULAR WALKS IN THE PEAK DISTRICT
LONG CIRCULAR WALKS IN THE PEAK DISTRICT
CIRCULAR WALKS IN WESTERN PEAKLAND
SHORT CIRCULAR WALKS IN THE STAFFORDSHIRE MOORLANDS
SHORT CIRCULAR WALKS AROUND THE TOWNS AND VILLAGES OF
THE PEAK DISTRICT
SHORT CIRCULAR WALKS AROUND MATLOCK
SHORT CIRCULAR WALKS IN THE DUKERIES
SHORT CIRCULAR WALKS IN SOUTH YORKSHIRE
SHORT CIRCULAR WALKS AROUND DERBY
SHORT CIRCULAR WALKS AROUND BAKEWELL
SHORT CIRCULAR WALKS AROUND BUXTON
SHORT CIRCULAR WALKS AROUND NOTTINGHAMSHIRE
SHORT CIRCULAR WALKS ON THE NORTHERN MOORS
40 SHORT CIRCULAR PEAK DISTRICT WALKS
SHORT CIRCULAR WALKS IN THE HOPE VALLEY

INSTRUCTION & RECORD -

HIKE TO BE FIT .... STROLLING WITH JOHN
THE JOHN MERRILL WALK RECORD BOOK

CANAL WALK GUIDES -

VOL ONE — DERBYSHIRE AND NOTTINGHAMSHIRE
VOL TWO — CHESHIRE AND STAFFORDSHIRE
VOL THREE — STAFFORDSHIRE
VOL FOUR — THE CHESHIRE RING
VOL FIVE — LINCOLNSHIRE & NOTTINGHAMSHIRE
VOL SIX — SOUTH YORKSHIRE
VOL SEVEN — THE TRENT & MERSEY CANAL

DAY CHALLENGE WALKS -

JOHN MERRILL'S WHITE PEAK CHALLENGE WALK
JOHN MERRILL'S YORKSHIRE DALES CHALLENGE WALK
JOHN MERRILL'S NORTH YORKSHIRE MOORS CHALLENGE WALK
PEAK DISTRICT END TO END WALKS
THE LITTLE JOHN CHALLENGE WALK
JOHN MERRILL'S LAKELAND CHALLENGE WALK
JOHN MERRILL'S STAFFORDSHIRE MOORLAND CHALLENGE WALK
JOHN MERRILL'S DARK PEAK CHALLENGE WALK

MULTIPLE DAY WALKS -

THE RIVERS' WAY
PEAK DISTRICT HIGH LEVEL ROUTE
PEAK DISTRICT MARATHONS
THE LIMEY WAY
THE PEAKLAND WAY

COAST WALKS -

ISLE OF WIGHT COAST WALK
PEMBROKESHIRE COAST PATH
THE CLEVELAND WAY

HISTORICAL GUIDES -

DERBYSHIRE INNS
HALLS AND CASTLES OF THE PEAK DISTRICT & DERBYSHIRE
TOURING THE PEAK DISTRICT AND DERBYSHIRE BY CAR
DERBYSHIRE FOLKLORE
LOST INDUSTRIES OF DERBYSHIRE
PUNISHMENT IN DERBYSHIRE
CUSTOMS OF THE PEAK DISTRICT AND DERBYSHIRE
WINSTER — A VISITOR'S GUIDE
ARKWRIGHT OF CROMFORD
TALES FROM THE MINES by GEOFFREY CARR
PEAK DISTRICT PLACE NAMES by MARTIN SPRAY

JOHN'S MARATHON WALKS -

TURN RIGHT AT LAND'S END
WITH MUSTARD ON MY BACK
TURN RIGHT AT DEATH VALLEY
EMERALD COAST WALK

COLOUR GUIDES -

THE PEAK DISTRICT...................................Something to remember her by.

SKETCH BOOKS — by John Creber

NORTH STAFFORDSHIRE SKETCHBOOK

CALENDARS

1989 JOHN MERRILL PEAK DISTRICT WALK A MONTH CALENDAR

adges are 3" in diameter; blue cloth with a walking boot
mbroidered in two colours.

BADGE ORDER FORM

ate completed ....

ime ....

NAME ....

DDRESS ....

....

rice: **£2.00 each including postage, VAT and signed completion**
ertificate.

rom: **J.N.M. Publications, Winster, Matlock, Derbyshire, DE4
DQ**
el: **Winster (062988) 454 — 24hr answering service.**

★★★ **You may photocopy this form if needed** ★★★★★

HE JOHN MERRILL WALK BADGE — **walk this route twice or
omplete another John Merrill's challenge walks and send
etails and cheque/PO for £2.00 for a special circular walk
adge. Price includes postage and VAT.**

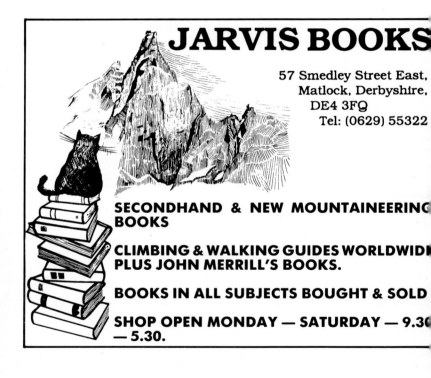